Today is a Snowy Day

by Martha E. H. Rustad

raintree

a Capstone company — publishers for children

Raintree is an imprint of Capstone Global Library Limited, a company incorporated in England and Wales having its registered office at 264 Banbury Road, Oxford, OX2 7DY – Registered company number: 6695582

www.raintree.co.uk
myorders@raintree.co.uk

Text © Capstone Global Library Limited 2017
The moral rights of the proprietor have been asserted.

Edited by Marissa Kirkman
Designed by Charmaine Whitman and Peggie Carley
Picture research by Tracey Engel
Production by Katy LaVigne
Originated by Capstone Global Library
Printed and bound in China.

ISBN 978 1 4747 3872 9
20 19 18 17 16
10 9 8 7 6 5 4 3 2 1

British Library Cataloguing in Publication Data
A full catalogue record for this book is available from the British Library.

Acknowledgements
We would like to thank the following for permission to reproduce photographs: Capstone: 6; iStockphoto: AwakenedEye, 18 (top left); Shutterstock: BlueSkyImage, cover, JNaether, 12, jordache, 1, 16, Kathy Ritter, 14, Kichigin, 8, kristinasavkov, 18 (design element), Kseniia Neverkovska, cover and interior design element, Max Topchii, 10, MNStudio, 4, Sergey Novikov, 20, -strizh-, cover and interior design element

Every effort has been made to contact copyright holders of material reproduced in this book. Any omissions will be rectified in subsequent printings if notice is given to the publisher.

All the internet addresses (URLs) given in this book were valid at the time of going to press. However, due to the dynamic nature of the internet, some addresses may have changed, or sites may have changed or ceased to exist since publication. While the author and publisher regret any inconvenience this may cause readers, no responsibility for any such changes can be accepted by either the author or the publisher.

Contents

What is the weather like?

Today is a snowy day.

Snowflakes float down gently.

We look at the forecast.

It tells us how much snow will fall.

How a snowflake forms

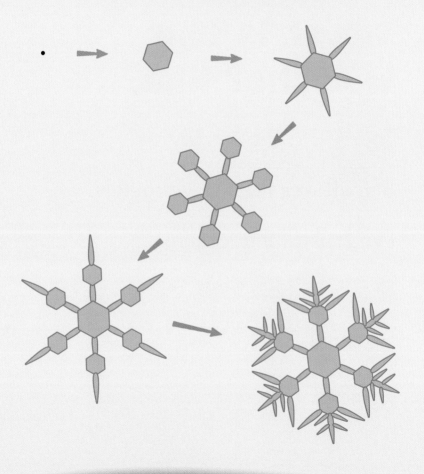

Snowflakes form in clouds.

Tiny bits of water freeze

around specks of dirt.

The snowflakes become heavy

and fall from the clouds.

Each snowflake looks different.

They freeze in different patterns.

Some flakes are bigger,

and some are smaller.

What do we see?

We see snow all around us.

Snowflakes land on buildings,

trees and on the ground.

The snow piles up.

A blanket of white covers everything.

We see footprints in the snow.

Animals leave tracks in the snow.

Cars also leave tracks.

We watch a snowplough

clear the road.

A snowy day sometimes turns into a blizzard. Strong, fast winds blow snow around. It can be hard to see anything outside. It is very cold. We stay safe inside.

What do we do?

We play outside on a snowy day.

We wear coats, waterproof trousers,

hats and gloves. We cover

our skin to keep it warm

and dry. Let's sledge downhill.

Amount of snow in centimetres

We measure how much snow has fallen. We use a measuring stick. We write down the amount on a chart. We see a pattern. Winter has the most snowy days.

We shovel the snow from
the pavement. Then we go inside
to warm up. We drink hot cocoa.
Look at the snowman we built!
Let's check the forecast for tomorrow.

Glossary

blizzard storm with fast winds and blowing snow

forecast prediction of what the weather will be

freeze to go from a liquid to a solid; water freezes at 0 degrees Celsius (32 degrees Fahrenheit)

pattern several things that are repeated in the same way each time

shovel tool used for lifting and clearing snow or dirt

Find out more

Books

A Snowstorm Shows Off: Blizzards (Bel the Weather Girl), Belinda Jensen (Millbrook Press, 2016)

Snow (Weather Wise), Helen Cox Cannons (Raintree, 2015)

What Can You See in Winter? (Seasons), Sian Smith (Raintree, 2015)

Websites

easyscienceforkids.com/how-is-snow-made/
Visit this site to learn fun facts about snow and watch a video of how snow is formed.

kidshealth.org/en/kids/winter-safety.html
Learn safety tips for cold winter weather.

www.weatherwizkids.com/?page_id=62
Learn all about winter storms and find directions to perform your own winter science experiments.

Index

Note to parents and teachers

The What is the Weather Today? series supports National Curriculum requirements for science related to weather. This book describes and illustrates a snowy day. The images support early readers in understanding the text. The repetition of words and phrases helps early readers learn new words. This book also introduces early readers to subject-specific vocabulary words, which are defined in the Glossary section. Early readers may need assistance to read some words and to use the Contents, Glossary, Find out more and Index sections of the book.